Thomas Salmon, John Birchensha, Stephen Monteage

An Essay to the Advancement of Musick

Thomas Salmon, John Birchensha, Stephen Monteage

An Essay to the Advancement of Musick

ISBN/EAN: 9783337225773

Printed in Europe, USA, Canada, Australia, Japan

Cover: Foto ©Thomas Meinert / pixelio.de

More available books at **www.hansebooks.com**

AN
ESSAY

To the Advancement of

MUSICK,

BY

Cafting away the Perplexity of

DIFFERENT CLIFFS.

And Uniting all forts of Mufick

Lute,	Organ,
Viol,	Harpfechord,
Violin,	Voice, &c.

In one Univerfal Chara&ter.

By THOMAS SALMON, *Mafter of Arts of* Trinity College *in* Oxford.

Fruftra fit per plura, quod fieri poteft per pauciora.

LONDON,
'rinted by *J. Macock,* and are to be Sold by
John Car at the *Middle-Temple-Gate.* 1672.

THE
PUBLISHER
TO THE
READER.

Courteous Reader,

THere is not any Art
which at this day is
more Rude, Unpo-
lish'd, and Imperfect,
in the Writings of most of the Ancient and Modern Authors, than
Musick; for the Elementary part
thereof, is little better than an
indigested Mass, and confused
Chaos of impertinent Characters,
and insignificant Signs.

It is intricate and difficult to be
understood; it afflicts the memory,

A 3 and

and *cònfumeth much time, before the knowledge thereof can be attained*: *Becaufe* the Cliffs are divers ; their Tranfpofition frequent ; the Order and places of Notes very mutable; and their denominations alterable and unfixed.

Thefe things being confidered by the Ingenious Author of this Book, (who endeavoureth only a reformation of the Regulative Principles of Practical Mufick) he hath here prefented thee with an Expedient, for the redrefs of thefe Obftacles, which do hinder the Practitioners of this Art from arriving in convenient time, at the end of their Labours ; which is, Perfection in the knowledge and Performance of Mufick.

Perfpicuity and Brevity facilitate : And here is a well-defigned Epitome

To the Reader.

Epitome of Practical Musick. For by this happy contrivance, the Cliffs, which were many, are reduced into an Univerfal Character ; the various fhifting of Notes in a Syfteme, or ftaff of lines are fixed : the neceffity of their Tranfpofitions taken away ; So that he that can Sing or Play any one Part, may Sing and Play all Parts ; And he that fhall know his diftances in any one Part, may know them in all Parts.

And fo great will the Benefit of this Effay be, to thofe who will make ufe of it, that I don't know what to requeft more advantageous for its acceptance, than an Experiental tryal. Reader, I fhall therefore think it needlefs to treat you with an Apology, where your advantage is like to be proportio-
nable

nable to your pains. And truly *you will find such pleasant variety,* *and profitable Novelty, that I am* *confident every Ingenious Musi-* *cian will be satisfied with his* *entertainment, sufficient both for* *his Phansie and Judgment.*

There can be *no* true Lover of Musick, *but will be favourable to* *the arguings, for its* institution and advantages : *No* Induſtrious Scholar, *but will congratulate his* knowledge, enlarged by an Uni- verſal Character. *No* Faithful Maſters, *but will* rejoyce *at, ra-* *ther than* envy the facility and advancement thereof. *Nay fur-* *ther, will certainly* applaud *the* *Propoſal* ; where that which makes the advantage, makes it alſo eaſie , and requires but half the pains to double the Accom- pliſhment. *Wherefore, I hope, that* they

To the Reader.

they, who at present are the most glorious in their attained difficulties, and so firm to that Practice, which for want of a better, is at present received; will, when they have experience of this way, consult their own Ease and Agreement with it.

This I was willing to premise, lest the out-crys of some should prepossess the Reader with a Practical impossibility; notwithstanding the Proposal is most evident and plain. Which moved me to be very earnest with this Gentleman, to give me this opportunity of being serviceable to all true Lovers of Musick, to whom there is none more devoted, than

Their Humble Servant

John Birchensha.

The Contents of the Chapters, and Advantages which arife from this Effay.

CHAP. I.

MUfick truly valued from its Authentick Creator; its Ancient Patronage, and that proper faculty, which was created for its reception. (Page 1. 2, 3.) The Advantages whereby it excells all other recreations in beft accomplifbing its performers, and re-difpofing them for any employment, (Page 6.)

CHAP. II.

The Scale of Mufick reduced to feven Notes, encircling themfelves in feveral Octaves, expreffed by the feven firft Letters of the Alphabet. (P. 11.) Whence it follows, That the hard names of the Gamut, and its conjuring repetition backwards and forwards, become unneceffary;

The Contents.

neceſſary; and the perplexed computing of Conſonant Notes are brought
to one plain account.

CHAP. III.

The ſame ſeven Notes and their O-
ƈaves are ever ſituated upon the ſame
lines and ſpaces. (Page 23.) *So that*
we have no troubleſome variety of
ſigned keys, none of their perplexed
Tranſpoſitions; but a conſtant and
Univerſal Character, the ſame in all
parts of Muſick upon all Inſtruments.
Hence alſo it follows, he that knows
his Notes in one part, knows them in
all parts.

CHAP. IV.

The Deſign Applyed.
I. *To Compoſition; that the conſonant*
and diſſonant intervals, being ever ſitu-
ated upon the ſame places in all the ſe-
veral Parts. (Page 32.) You may
more clearly perceive which they be,
and where they are to be written
down.

II.

The Contents.

CHAP. V.

The Contents.

II. *To the Viol, where the different Cliffs being laid aside, and the Notes rightfully inheriting the places of their Octaves.* (Page 46.) There is not half the time and pains required to be perfect in the book as formerly; and he that shall, or can already play only by the pricking of the Base; shall be able to play the higher parts; and whatsoever was writ for any other Musick, which ever conforms it self to this its constant foundation.

An Universal Tuning proposed for the Viol, (Page 51.) *whereby it is made capable,* at once to express the melody of a Lyra tuning, and the intelligence of Notes.

III. *To the Organ, Harpsechord, or Virginals; in which all things are carried by the exact resemblance of Octaves, as the eye may most readily apprehend them, both upon the Book and Instrument,* (Page 57.) *whereby we avoid,* 1. The perplexed care of different Cliffs for each hand at the same time. 2. The invincible difficulties of their arbitrary transposition. 3. That distracting multiplicity of six or more lines, which are here reduced to five.

IV. *To*

The Contents.

The Contents.

2. He may by the Scheme propofed, write any Leſſons of the preſent
Tableture, into Notes, for the Harpfecord or any other Muſick.

3. He may take any Treble and
Baſe, which were deſigned for any
other Muſick, and play them upon the
Lute. *And,*

4. Hath broke Priſon, and may by
this uſe of Notes, come to arrive at
perfection in compoſing for, as well
as playing upon this ſupream Muſick.

*None of which could in the leaſt be
done, though one practiſed an hundred
years by letters.*

CHAP. VI.

The Objections Anſwered, (Pag.74.)

The Concluſion.

*A Compendious review of a Learners
task, being only the knowledge of the
ſame ſeven Notes in ſeveral Octaves upon the Inſtrument, by the ſeven firſt
Letters of the* Alphabet, *ever applyed to
the ſame ſeven places upon the Book.*
(Page 85.) So that for all the fore-
mentioned

The Contents.

mentioned advantages, there is but half the pains required, which people take to be without them.

The Neceſſity of a Maſter, *the Advantage from the moſt* Skilful, *who is intreated to favour his Scholars requeſts, and perfect their accompliſhments,* by a generous diſcovery of the nature and compoſition of *Muſick*; (Page 88.) *which might be eaſily brought to paſs* by their conduct, and a good *Muſical ingeny.*

ERRATA.

PAge 4. line 12. for Nations, read *Notions,* p. 6. l. 9. for now, r. *new,* p. 7. l. 20. for repair, r. *require,* p. 11. l. 2. for verifies, r. *terrifies,* p. 11. l. 5. for fictions, r. *fictitious,* p. 14. l. 28. for iet, r. *ſet.*

THE

AN
ESSAY
TO THE
Advancement of Musick.

CHAP. I.

The Advantages of Musick.

Mongſt theſe many Re-
creations which ſweeten
the life of man, and with
a pleaſing variety refreſh
his wearied mind ; none
can plead more advantages, or more
truly juſtifie it's practice, than Muſick ;
which needs nothing elſe, nor can
have any thing greater to command
acceptance, then a challenge of it's in-
ſtitution from Divine Providence it
B ſelf:

felf: For upon this account God hath created a peculiar faculty of hearing, to receive harmonious founds, clearly different from that by which we perceive ordinary noifes; infomuch, that thofe who have not this Mufical hearing, are by Nature as uncapable to underftand Harmony, as a Horfe is to receive the civility of a Complement. And indeed as each particular fenfe is fubordinate to, but diftinct from the common; fo here is fome fpecifick power which fub-divides this more private faculty from the common nature of hearing: Or elfe what can be the reafon, why all men that have ears enough to entertain founds in general, fhould not be able to difcern the pleafure of Mufick (which is a combination of founds as they are proportioned in numbers) but becaufe they want that faculty which is fitted with a peculiar power for their reception.

He that hath any one fenfe good, is capable of all objects that fall under fuch a fenfe; one that can fee a horfe, may fee a houfe, but he that can tell a clock, cannot always tell the movements of a leffon, and the Harmony of its confenting parts, which is the object
of

of a more special power. Neither can this be thought to proceed only from a more nice acuteness of the ear, since that several persons, who betray much deafness in their common discourse and converse, are able exactly to Tune their Musical Instruments, and discover the jarring of any dissonant note, though but softly pronounced: Whereby it appears that this peculiar faculty doth not meerly arise from an excellency of the common hearing, and consequently that they are not the same. But whether the distinction comes from a different formation of the little intrigues of the ear, or only from an improvement that some mens souls are able to make of sounds so qualifyed and represented to them; it is hard to determine, and needless for my purpose, so long as we find *de facto*, that there is such a Musical hearing, and that God hath given some men such a particular faculty, wheresoever it pleased him to place it.

Now lest this faculty should seem to be any time created in vain, Holy Writ but succinctly describing the infancy of the world, yet vouchsafes to mention Jubal, the Musical Father of

thofe

those who handle the Harp and Organ.

So that whosoever shall consider the Authentick creator of Musick, it's antient Patronage, and moreover, the practice of all civilized Nations, yet shall condemn it as silly and trifling, as unworthy of generous and heroick minds; not only slight those reasons which obtain in far greater matters, but also betray themselves to be ignorant of those exalted Nations, and noble Sentiments, which make it honoured both in Peace and War: And indeed to have so little ingenuity, that they can never apprehend its excellency, wherefore they neglect what is above them, and take up with some rustick pastime which is common to Clowns and Fools.

Now to enumerate the Advantages Musick hath above other divertisements, it is necessary to alledge its incomparable pleasure, which makes it the greatest recreation; but because that is only known by hearing, and its self best expresses its own sweet eloquence, I must remit you to its practical and delicious entertainments, where you shall seldom meet with people so rude,

be known nature hath denied them.
Though you fhall have fome men fo
importunate to fhew themfelves wits,
and tell ftories of the great Turks im-
patience, that they will break out in
the midft of a fuit of leffons, and
then call for Bobbing Jone, or the
Nightingale; as if their brisk fancies
were not to be damped with the gravity of an Almain, and they knew
better from their Countrey Scrapers,
then what thefe troublefom Contrivers
of Confort perplex them with.

It may feem impertinent to prove a
recreation profitable, or to refpect intereft in the choice of pleafure; but
that gain is fuch a taking thing in the
world, as if we can make out Mufick
in this kind advantageous to the pra-
cticer, it will be treated with a double
welcom. To this purpofe let us but a
little confider other Sports, as Cards,
Tables, Chefs, &c. and you will find
that its expences may be efteemed
good husbandry, though for its excellency it deferves to be purchafed by
the greateft charge, fince by its refrefh-

ing

ing sweetneſs it lulls the ſoul into its own pacate poſture, and gives eaſe and quiet; when other games in their diverſion only rack and torment it. But let us purſue the compariſon.

1. Thoſe are meer paſtimes, which when we have ſpent many hours in frequenting, do not rediſpoſe us to undertake now buſineſs, but leave the head hot, the faculties tired, and the man quite diſabled to ſtudy or work; whereas his recreation ought to fit him for it; but after the hearing ſome briſk Airs, or melodious Conſort, the mind is raiſed, the fancy enlivened, care and ſorrow ſuppreſſed, and an inclination produced ready to diſpatch any employment. Such a noble power hath Muſick over the ſoul; which though it is not (as *Plato* thought) only Harmony; yet Harmony may claim very great acquaintance with it, ſince 'twas uſed as a ſacred means to allay *Sauls* anger; and doth ſtill ſet the Soul in order, charming the madneſs even of one bitten by a Tarantula.

But to the pleaſure and preparation for buſineſs, there is another profit ſuperadded, that when one hath ſpent

ſome

some hours in this Recreation, he hath attain'd an Art, which where-ever the person comes, shall bring him in esteem, and create a delight to the society he is in; whilst what glory is it to shuffle and cut the Cards well? or dexterously to jog the elbow, unless in a discreditable phrase? and I don't doubt but this argument will be valued amongst those that are ingeniously covetous of accomplishments.

2. The charges of this recreation are much less then of others; for no Gamester will play, unless his wager be considerable enough to oblige his attention; if then we suppose a Gentleman to keep within moderate bounds (so he plays like himself) he may easily lose more in one night, then his Musick will repair for a month; but how often doth a bewitching passion prevail to double the stakes, and then venture at all, till at last a cross cast ruines his estate, and miserably destroys a Noble Family; many sad examples can prove Gaming guilty of this: but though Musick was never famous for enriching men, it was never known to have begger'd any.

I am perfwaded that were the minds of our Englifh youth, more poffeffed with this delightful and innocent recreation, which is hardly capable of excefs, they would afterwards value it above their vainer Sports, and by their efteem and pleafure in it, be fore-ftalled againft any extravagant debauchery. It may therefore upon this account feem a more ingenious piece of policy, for fome progging Guardians to educate their Pupils in this advantageous divertifement, rather then to inftill their fneaking principles of covetoufnefs, which if they take effect, render them bafe on one hand, but ofteneft on the other break out into a contradictive prodigality; as we daily fee the moft fubtle fcraping fellows are ufually followed by the wildeft heirs.

In Country Recreations (which Citizens enjoy not, neither are like Mufick, always in feafon, but depend much upon the time of the year, and the weather) there is not much to be valued, except the wholfome exercife, and the frefh air, which are things altogether extrinfical, in refpect of the Sport, whofe quarry is always unworthy
thy

thy fo great pains, and the charges of maintenance without proportion. Many a Gentleman hath had his eftate devoured by his ravenous Hawks, and undergone the fate of *Acteon*, who ftill remains an emblem of thofe Hunters, that have been eaten up by their own dogs.

I know nothing that can be alledged againft Mufick, but that it is too fedentary and unactive; which (if it fhould be fo) is no more then the forementioned unprofitable Games, may be juftly accufed of; yet being further confidered, it may vie wholfomnefs with the beft; for there is nothing fo efficacioufly opens the breaft, as Singing, which exercifes the Lungs, and confequently puts the blood into a brisker motion, whilft fome warbling thrill, ftrains thofe parts, and affifts in the feparation of the fluggifh flegm: They that practice on the Viol, are able to overcome the cold of a Winters morning, and excite a ruddy warmth, which, by Phyficians, is fet as the boundary of an wholfom exercife.

After all thefe Advantages of Mufick, which is fo noble and gentile, that

it

it may not unbecome the higheſt honour or moſt ſerious gravity. I could not but admire the Learning was ſo little frequented, and the exerciſe leſs, but obſerving how many in vain attempted its dark and tedious principles; how many more were utterly diſcouraged by the ill ſucceſs of others; I found it was the difficulty lay in the way, and hindred acceſs to this, as it does to all other brave accompliſhments. Wherefore the deſign of theſe Papers is to take away the affrighting bug-bear terms, to reduce the confuſed cliffs into one eſtabliſhed order; and if there be any faith had to reaſon and experience, to ſhow a way for the attainment of Muſick by Notes, in much leſs then the uſual time required.

CHAP.

CHAP. II.

The Gamut Reformed.

THat which firſt of all verifies a beginner, is a long diſcourſe of Gibberiſh, a Fardle of hard names and fictious words called the Gamut, preſented to him perfectly to be learned without book, till he can readily repeat it backwards and forwards; as though a man muſt be exact in the Art of Conjuring before he might enter upon Muſick. But I am certain if he can ſay *G, A, B, C, D, E, F, G,* it will do to all intents and purpoſes as well. For the plain truth is, there are but ſeven Notes in all, only repeated over and over again in a double and treble proportion.

That an Octave is meerly a Note doubled, any Muſitian will tell you, and a man may eaſily ſatisfie himſelf, if he will but ſtop with his finger in the middle of a ſtring; for he ſhall then find, that either of thoſe two parts will be an Octave to the ſtring open. This alſo *Kircher* in his *Muſurgia,* proves by an ingenious experiment; take

take two drinking glaffes (faith he)
and fill one half way with water, and
the other with the like quantity of
fome groffer liquor, juft of a double
thicknefs, then draw your finger
pretty ftiff about the brim of the
glaffes feveral times, till the parts are
put in motion, and you will hear a
Mufical murmuring of Octaves from
thefe new kind of glafs inftruments.

An Octave therefore being the fame,
in all refpects with its original Note,
like fome beloved Son, who is the
pretty Picture of his Parent, and will
ferve at any time in his Fathers abfence; it will be the fame thing, if after I have paffed one Octave, I begin
a new to reckon the reft, and fo round,
as if I afcended in the prefent variety
from eight to fifteen, and fo to two
and twenty. Hence I make my Scale
or Mufical Ladder but feven rounds
high, which, while I make three or
four feveral marks for as many different Octaves one higher then another,
fhall be able to reach the talleft Note
in Mufick; for it will be all one, and
much more perfpicuous to fay a fifth
in the fecond Octave, than a twelfth
that is D la fol re, is an Octave and a
fifth

fifth from *Gamut*, than (which is the same) twelve Notes diftant.

And now you may difcern the conveniency of this way of accounting for a young Compofer, will much fooner ken the Intervals of feven Notes only, then if they were continued up to thirty; efpecially if you confider how the Muficians reckon inclufively, as if eight and eight were fifteen, and eight more two and twenty, which makes the intermediate Concords lie after this rate much at randome. I confefs if Mufick divided it felf by tens, as fuppofe eight fhould have for its equivalent concords eighteen, and eight and twenty; this would be a good clear way to reckon our Notes, but fince in refpect of *Gamut*, or the Note from whence we reckon, a third, a tenth, a feventeenth are the three B's, or Notes of the fame compofing value, we make a very confufed computation, which would be avoided by the round about of an Octave.

I will give you one true and moft evident comparifon; the Muficians at prefent reckon their Notes at length, as the *Jews* of old did their months by a continued number of days; but as

our cuſtom is eaſier, which computes
them by weeks, and comes about a-
gain with the ſame days, and the ſame
number of days, ſo with great facility
ſhall I caſt up my Muſical account
within the circulation of an Octave;
for it will be all one if I ſay, I will do
a thing one and twenty days hence, or
this day three weeks; and beſides, I
eſcape the difficulty fore-mentioned,
that lies in the croſs ſituation of equivalent Notes.

That thoſe foreſaid hard names are
nothing to the purpoſe; I thus prove
it; for they ſhould either diſtinguiſh
what Octave the Note is in, or ſignifie
the placing of Mi.

1. They can't declare a Note to be
in a different Octave, becauſe their
names are not different in every O-
ctave; as that F ſa ut is always the
ſame, and G ſol re ut, *Alamire* and moſt
of the reſt differ not in the upper
Octaves: Wherefore really to diſtinguiſh them, I will at the beginning of
every leſſon in the place of three (in
themſelves inſignificant) cliff characters, iet thoſe letters which expreſs
the part wherein the Muſick is plac'd;
as B for the baſe, ſo called (and ought

to

to be writ) becaufe it is the Bdns or
foundation of Mufick.   M for the
mean or middle part; Tr. for the treble, and if it be requifite to ufe the
Notes in Alt, you may for an higher
Octave put double Ttr.

2. If the fictitious words of the *Gamut* were originally defigned to fhew
the place of Mi, yet muft they now be
ufelefs for this end alfo, becaufe Re
and Ut, which chiefly compofe thefe
feigned names, are by Englifh Muficians already laid afide; fo that I can't
tell any thing that perfwades *Muſick-
Maſters* to trouble their Scholars with
an *impertinent difficulty*, but *a pernici-
ous humour in fome men* ftill to do what
hath once been done, howfoever ufelefs and unprofitable; or elfe an opini-
on that Mufick will appear in the
greater grandeur by bearing fuch my-
fterious terms in the front.

But how ever the *Gamut* hath been
ftill continued, the Muficians themfelves have thought it infufficient for
the purpofe alledged.   Wherefore
that we may know how to place Mi,
they give us this rule which always
holds good, *viz.* before Mi afcending
to name fa, fol, la, mi, and after mi de-
scending,

scending, mi, la, sol, fa. Now that which they are to be blamed for in this is, that when they have given their Scholars a Notional understanding of this direction, their practice is to take their rise from sol, and sing sol, la, mi, fa, sol, la, fa, sol; as though sol was the syllable from whence they should take aim, by which means they never perfect their main rule; and so as Mi alters, are confounded in naming their Notes; whereas, if in their practice they begin with mi, and so sing forwards, mi, fa, sol, la, fa, sol, la, mi; they would at once learn to rise an Octave with their voice, and gain a readiness in this rule, which they are always to account by in whatever condition they find Mi.

It is to no purpose to plead that sol is for the most part in *the cliff line*, and therefore ready to begin with as they go upward; because these syllables are practiced only in order to other Singing; now Songs begin not with sol, and go forward in that method, but upon any note, and so skip about, that no rule can be observed, but that which we contend for always to be practised.

I

*I shall new present you with the Old and
New Gamut.*

The Old Gamut.

E	la		
D	la	fol	
C	fol	fa	
B	fa	b	mi
A	la	mi	re
G	fol	re	ut
F	fa	ut	
E	la	mi	
D	la	fol	re
C	fol	fa	ut
B	fa	b	mi
A	la	mi	re
G	fol	re	ut
F	fa	ut	
E	la	mi	
D	fol	re	
C	fa	ut	
B	mi		
A	re		
gamut			

The New Gamut.

G. A. B. C. D. E. F. G.

C

We are fure, what we have under-
took, is fufficiently proved, that
G, A, B, C, D, E, F, G, will do as well
as the old hard names; and for the
placing of Mi, you muft take the ufual Monofyllables, fo you order them
in the moft practicable method, *viz.*
Mi fa fol la fa fol la mi.

I come now to my chief Defign,
which is, the Reduction of Cliffs into
one eftablifhed Order : whofe clear
and facile Method, will fo bribe the
Practitioner; and whofe *Univerfal
Character* will afford him fuch Catholick converfe in Mufick, that I don't
doubt, but being ftrengthened by fo
great Conveniencies, it will be able to
graple with any imputation of Fancy
and Novelty.

CHAP.

CHAP. III.

The Cliffs reduced to one Univerfal Character.

THAT intolerable perplexity which arofe from the Alteration of Cliffs, caufed fome charitable, but lazy Wit, to invent Tableture; whereby the Notes are Mechanically clouded in Letters, and fo darkly, that the moft quick-fighted Mufick-mafter himfelf, can't tell what they mean, till he finds out the Tuning of the Inftrument, and then produces the Sound; which if expreffed in Notes, might be underftood at firft view: whilft that the Scholar who is this way inftructed, is condemned ever to be ignorant of the rational part of his Mufick; and never to Play any thing, but what he hath practifed before; or elfe is well acquainted with the humour of it.

For the Voice, and thofe Inftruments that are not able to be expreffed by Letters, people learn by rote, and quickly forget again, what like Parrots they ignorantly prated. I would

there-

therefore by one steady settlement,
bring Notes to be as easie as Letters;
and so introduce our fore-mentioned
Practitioners into a more understanding ways as also to save that Infinite
Expence of Time and Trouble, which
some Lovers of Musick were content
to undergo.

The present Practice is to make
three Cliffs, whose Notes, by which
they are called, are a fifth above one
another; and according to the most
conveniency in writing, are usually
assigned to their places in the Scheme.

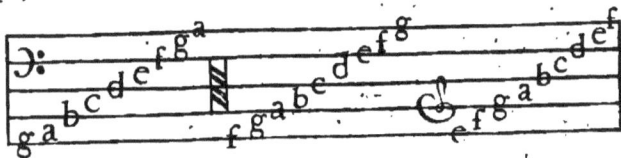

Where you first learn to know the
Notes in such a different situation,
that sometimes the lowermost line is g.
sometimes f. sometimes e. and consequently all other lines and spaces
suffer the like perplexed variety.
Where, who can conceive how great
the difficulty must be, if from only
observing the Cliff Notes at the beginning of the line, we must suddenly,
but

but exactly, know the Intervals of all
the Notes; however they skip and
jump to the end of the Leſſon: or
elſe have the lines and ſpaces ſo clearly
fixed in our heads, that, without any
Computation, we may apprehend them
as barely ſituated in the three-fold difference.

And after all this is attained (which
one would think inſuperable; but that
many years practice, and the vaſt
pleaſure of Muſick, hath been able to
overcome any thing) you muſt, from
the ſuppoſition of placing any one
Note in any place, by a quick way of
reaſon, argue the ſituation of all the
reſt, diſordered by the Tranſpoſition
of the figned Keys.

Which difficulty and confuſion appears, by the following Scheme.

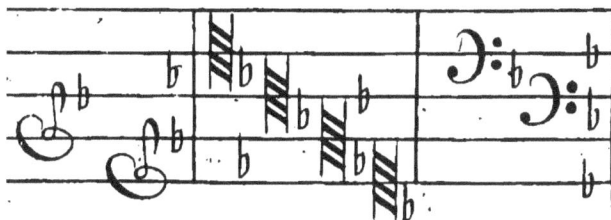

Treble   Meane   Baſe

For

For Mufick-mafters, that their Leffon may fall beft within the compafs
of five lines, place the Cliffs in any
line; by which means there are, in
truth, as many Cliffs as lines; and as
many alterations, as both lines and
fpaces can make.

Perhaps fome will fay, they only
obferve the Intervalls of following
Notes, and fo care not upon what lines
and fpaces they are fituated; which,
indeed, is the beft way as things are;
but this won't do. For no Scholar is
capable to make ufe of it under a years
practice, nor can a Mufick-mafter himfelf truft to it, in the paffage from one
Cliff to another. As when a Violift
paffes from F fa ut, to C fol fa ut
Cliff; the Notes muft not be plaid
according to their Intervall; but there
muft be a new aim taken from the
Cliff Character, as is already related.
Though this is fo far from thwarting
my Propofal, that if you follow it,
the laft Objection is taken away, and
the Intervalls will be always true; only in another Octave.

And now, I only fear, my Reader
fhould think me obfcure; whereas the
bufinefs, as it is now practifed, is fo
diffi-

difficult!, that I could hardly conceive it
my felf; and therefore, I doubt, have
not clearly explained the Confufion of
the former way of pricking.

I could not think it feafable to reduce thefe entangled perplexities into
one Order, or that fuch Pilgrim Notes
could be fixed in any conftant dwel-
lings, but that the following Contrivance fhews me it may, and is here
already accomplifhed.

The New Scheme for the conftant fituation
of the fame Notes, and their Octaves,
on the fame Lines and Spaces.

This upper line lies Lieger for the bufinefs of an higher Octaue.

Tr   g   a   b   c   d   e   f

Treble
The Lieger line

Tr   g   a   b   c   d   e   f

Treble
The Lieger line

M   g   a   b   c   d   e   f

Meane
The Lieger line

B   g   a   b   c   d   e   f

Bafe

As it is eafier to find a Man, who always keeps his home, than if he fpent his time in continual Rambling ; fo I fuppofe, none can deny, but the Notes may be more readily known, when they are perpetually rivited into the fame places , then if they were fhuffled up and down in their former Alteterations.

I would not therefore be tedious, in further purfuing fo plain a Demonftration, but that Mufick-mafters, who have by the practice of their whole Lives, attained this laborious Art; (this now troublefom and infignificant Excellency) will be loath to confent to a Way, wherein every young Practitioner may Rival them; who by exercifing himfelf only in that one Method propofed, fhall be as nimble at his Book, to play by fight in a year, as they are in an Age.

For do but fuppofe all the labour that was fpent in practifing three Cliffs, had been beftowed upon one; and that diftracted variety (which in perfecting one did, as it were, imperfect another) was contracted in our United Order, how great would the Perfection be. And let me tell you, though
the

the other way may serve for thofe, who, all their life time, and every day, make a trade of Mufick; yet, Gentlemen, who take it for a Recreation, and therefore muft difcontinue their practice as bufinefs requires, are never able to maintain fuch a knowledge, as confifts in confufion; and confequently, will be daily impaired, if at all omitted. And I can here plead the fad experience of this, which makes me fo zealous in the Remedy. For after I had with much trouble over-come the Diverfity of Cliffs, two or three months abfence from my Mufick, caft me into fuch a Relapfe, that I could fcarcely, in fo much time, recover them again.

Wherefore, having made this Propofal to fome Mufick-mafters; they returned me fuch Objections, as partly betrayed their mif-apprehenfions of my defign; but chiefly their unwillingnefs it fhould come into practice. Upon which account, I put my felf upon the trouble of writing thefe Papers; that they might the more clearly perceive the conveniency of this *Hypothefis*. And if afterwards they fhould remain peevifh, and obftinate

againft

againſt the uſe of it ; their Scholars
might be able to Right themſelves,
and demand a Remiſſion of more then
half their ſlaviſh task. For, to learn
the Notes, and Con their Places, is
the very Drudgery of Muſick. And
who is it that would be willing thus
to undergo a tedious half year, before he comes to enjoy, the delicious
ſweets of Conſort, if he knows how
to remedy ſo great a labour? And
whereas they told me it might do,
but would be never practiſed ; le:
them not take care for that ; when once
men find it will ſave them more then
half the Trouble, they will embrace
it as readily, as if I was Emperour of
the world to command it. For Conveniency is an Uuiverſal King.

It is the Intereſt of Muſicians to have
their Art underſtood ; for there is nothing ſo much its hinderance, as ignorance of its Excellency ; neither let
them think, that the ſooner Learned,
the ſooner left off ; for whereas many
faint in their firſt Eſſays, and others
contend to conquer it, ſo long only
as their patience will laſt ; if the way
was more plain, theſe might arrive at
ſome Perfection, and practiſe it ever
                                    after,

after, as the chief Recreation of their Lives.

But if after all this, Muſick-maſters ſhall double the time in teaching their Scholars, in hopes of double Gain; or their Scholars be ſuch Fools to under-go that Expence of Time and Trou-ble; give me leave to laugh, and let them have their labour for their pains.

CHAP.

CHAP. IV.

The Design Applyed; and first to Vocal Musick.

THAT this way may not seem an Airy Notion, or Speculative fancy at large, which is not capable of convenient practice: I shall now apply it to particular Musick, and shew that it will not only serve for all Instruments and Voices; but that some other considerable Advantages will accrue in every one of them. One thing of no small account, is, that whatsoever Musick is writ this way, is equally proper; and as I may say, peculiar to all manner of performances.

Suppose an Air thus prick'd; you may indifferently play it with French Lute, Theorb, Viol, or Violin, &c. or Sing it with either Base, or Treble Voice. The Players, indeed, will find it but in one, yet every ones Native Language (though I must acknowledge that the Dialects of Instruments are different) and the various Practitioners will admire their Instruments,

Har-

Harmonious in their Pricking too. Like that late ingeniously invented Univerſal Charaƈter, which, expreſſing things, and not words, is common to all Countries; and may be read by thoſe who agree not in ſpeaking, neither at all underſtand one anothers Diſcourſe.

I confeſs this might poſſibly be done by thoſe, who have perfeƈtly over-come the Difficulties related in the beginning of the laſt Chapter; but they are only the abſolute Maſters of Muſick; that when I ſay any Scholar who learns only upon one Inſtrument, ſhall be able to do it, as well as if he had learned of all. I may aſſert, that to be done by this, which could not be done before; and that to be brought into common uſe, which was ſcarcely in Speculation, except amongſt Muſick-maſters themſelves. How could one that learned only upon the Violin, and conſequently was exerciſed only in G ſol re ut Cliff, play an Air writ for the Viol in F fa ut, and C ſol fa ut? or a Voice that was uſed only to the Baſe, Sing a Tune in the Treble Cliff? *It neither was nor could be.* Wherefore it is much more advanta-
gious

gious for a Scholar, who, when he be-
gins, is indifferent to all, to learn this
way; by which, Mufick is brought to
fuch a general Confent, that from his
own Inftrument he underftands all o-
thers, and gains a Catholick knowledge in the Art.

Neither is this Propofal fit only for
the infancy of Mufick, or a device
fuited to young Beginners ; but it is
of as great ufe in Compofing, as Practice.

In many parts you fhall fee the Concords lye in fuch Order, and every
Harmonical Relation in fo plain a Method before your Eyes; that you may
perceive the Diftances of Notes at firft
view ; and without any laborious computing, be made privy to the whole
contrivance of Compofition.   For
here every Octave ftands upon the
fame Line; each Fifth, two Lines
higher ; and all the other Notes in fuch
like conftant refpect ; whilft as they
were before in the Syfteme of five
Lines , fometimes they ftood higher,
fometimes lower, and danced up and
down, according to the variation of
the Cliff.   Upon which account, Mafter *Sympfon,* perceiving it impoffible
for

for a Compofer to have ready enough
in his Eye, the Concords as they were
placed; and yet knowing it neceffary
for a man to carry in his mind, how
frequently he ufed his Diftances, left
two fifths, or two eighths come together, and many more inconveniencies;
He doth in his Book of Compofition,
advife a man to fet the Figures between the parts, whereby he may remember what Concords he hath, and
fhall for the future make ufe of; which
Mechanical Trouble is here taken
away.

*The following Scheme, on the
other fide, fhews the Intervalls
of all Notes in their conftant
fituation.*

And

T					
M					
B					

Greater 6ᵗʰ   Lesser 7ᵗʰ   Defect 8   Greater 7   8.

T					
M					
B					

4ᵗʰ   Imperfect 5ᵗʰ   Greater 4ᵗʰ   5   Lesser 6ᵗʰ

T					
M					
B					

Unison   Lesser 2ᵈ   Greater 2ᵈ   Lesser 3ᵈ   Greater 3ᵈ

*Thus all the Notes & their intervals are Situated in all parts whose
advantage & practicableness you may see in ỹ next cut of 8 parts.*

And as they are placed in one part,
so in every part; but (as you might
observe in my Explication of the
Gamut) according to the old way;
the Composer must be troubled to find
out his Concords, because they lye
cross in computing before he writes
them down : So that according to the
two former Hypothesis, I will make a
wild Comparison, how madly custom
perswades Musicians to reckon.

Upon *Thursday* the fourth of *Fe-
bruary*, suppose I write a Letter to my
Friend, and calling that day Gam ut;
I tell him, I will will give him a visit

Mr Simpson's Compend: P. 75.

is needless to set thited in the same respective dif=
ance as if there refferent Octave which also the
liffs (and more obf all or any of the Notes as the
liffs doe which bour included spaces doe demon=

on *Ela*, which happens to be *Shrove-Tuefday*, the three and twentieth of that month. He muft firft reckon how many Notes there are betwixt *Gamut*, and *Ela*, *viz.* twenty, inclufive. Then what Mufical proportion there is in that Interval; and afterwards Compute where to write it down. All this is done betwixt every Confonant Note;and almoft as much in the progrefs of every ftroke in a Leffon; whereas, if he had expreffed himfelf by the Notion of two Octaves and a Sixth; he would immediately have known, that the value of that Concord had been a Sixth; and with as much eafe underftood it, as the Gentleman would, if I had affigned my time by next *Tuefday* come three weeks.

But then if the Cliffs be moveable, he muft take aim according to their variation; juft as if to find the *Shrove-Tuefday* appointed; I muft reckon by the new Moons when *Eafter* fell; and fo learn that moveable Feaft. Though this may feem very extravagant, yet it is no more then the thing it felf; and in my judgment, I think it much harder to be perfect in the Cliffs, then to Calculate for Almanacks.   D   What-

Whatfoever is moſt natural, is always
moſt eaſie: Now, Nature her ſelf hath
made this Diviſion by Octaves; and after the compleating of them, brings her
Muſick into the ſame poſture; which aſ-
ſures me, that however uſe hath hi-
therto obtained to make five Notes
the diſtance of a Cliff, yet I have a good
Foundation to juſtifie my altering the
preſent way of writing; and to eſta-
bliſh it only by Octaves. I will tell
you a pretty Experiment of a Pipe,
or Flageolet, to this purpoſe; blow
with a ſoft, or gentle breath, one of the
lower Notes of the Pipe, and let the
ſtops remain the ſame, only encreaſing
your breath by degrees, and you ſhall
find, that no intermediate higher Note
will ſound, till at laſt it breaks forth
into an Octave.

Thus the voice doth naturally in-
cline to alter it ſelf by eight Notes,
and conſequently, will beſt conform
to the writing by this ſuppoſition,
though it underſtood not the change
upon a fifth; and therefore a Song
was always carried on in the ſame
Cliff it begun; yet if it ſhall be found
troubleſom to alter the Octave in the
middle of a Song, though eight Notes

be

be compleated in four lines, yet you
may write upon five or six; and as
you did before continue up the Notes;
which will be no trouble, if so be
you never make, nor change any Cliff;
for 'tis easier to find the Notes that are
fixed upon five or six lines, then
those that wander, and are uncertain
upon three.

I now begin with *Vocal Musick*,
whose worth justly giveth it the Pre-
heminence, and may claim Birth-
right from Nature, whose melodious
daughter it is. Instruments depend
upon Art for Contrivance, and still
require some trouble to relieve their
disorders : but this is always framed,
and ready tuned by its first Parent,
the Harmonious Engineer of the
world. And it pleaseth me well, that
the Musick, which is the most Excellent, should receive the greatest Advantages from this present Proposal;
for hereby we shall not only escape
the difficulty of Cliffs, and confequently much other trouble, which I
have hinted before, and is common
with the rest; but also attain a steady
settlement in the situation of *Mi.*

which

which is always neceſſary to be known, before we can name any of the other Notes, and will now be eaſily diſcerned and remembred ; ſince a regular flat can be only placed upon the ſecond line *B,* and the third ſpace *E* ; whereas heretofore *Mi* was ſo fickle and uncertain, that there was never a line or ſpace, but in ſome of the old ſigned *Cliffs* or other ; *B* flat, would intrude and diſpoſſeſs him of his ſeat.

‒ And by how much Muſicians have been wanton in their various *Cliffs* for Singing, (which is moſt of all perplexed with the manifold movements of *C ſol fa ut Cliff,* and the conſequent diſorders of *Mi*) they bring in evidence of the miſchief it makes; for where one Scholar learns to Sing or Play on the Harpſechord by Notes, ten do on the Viol and Violin.

And, indeed, all grave and ſolemn Muſick, hath thereby become ſo intricate and troubleſom, that for eaſe ſake, many Gentlemen had given themſelves over to whiſtling and fidling upon the Violin and Flageolet, till they were ſo rival'd by their Lacques and Barbers boys, that they were
                                    forc'd

forc'd to quit them, as Ladies do their fashions, when the Chamber-maids have inherited their old cloaths.

But that you may see how unneceſſary thoſe former various *Cliffs* are, how conveniently a Song will fall in the Syſteme of five lines (for though an Octave is compleated in four, yet you may take ſuch a liberty) written according to our Hypotheſis of every part beginning with *G*, in the lowermoſt line. I have given you an example of a Song in Four Parts, compoſed by the Eminent, and Ingenious Mr. *Humphries*, where you may obſerve the concords keep an exact reſpect to one another; the *B* flats always in the ſame lines and ſpaces, ſuch a pleaſant agreement and familiar likeneſs through the whole courſe of it, that at firſt view, you may diſcern what kindred and relation there is betwixt every conſenting Note, *viz.* all the Octaves ſtanding upon the ſame lines and ſpaces, the fifths two higher, *&c.* proportionably after the ſame manner.

Here insert the Plate for the Song Aurelia.

D 3

In

In all writing you muſt ſtrictly obſerve to aſſign that Octave, to which
the Notes do moſt properly belong,
and in which they will be moſt com-
pactedly comprehended, and then it
will be very rare but the Songs will
conveniently fall within the compaſs
of the lines; and if otherwiſe they
ſhould prove'at any time unruly from
ſome enlarged fancies, yet there be
ſeveral ways to remedy their Efforts,
and comprehend their wideſt latitude, without any prejudice to our
Hypotheſis; nay, with greater advantage by it, than any other way; for beſides, the drawing an aſcititious line
over or under upon leſſer occaſions,
you may;

1. In any place, where the Notes
riſe or fall an Octave (which is uſually
the cauſe of greateſt diſtreſs in this
caſe) ſet the next Note in the ſame
place, only changing the letter of the
Octave, which will direct you to Sing
it an eight higher or lower; as you
may ſee theſe three Notes, which required three different Places, in three
different Cliffs, are here ſituated all
upon the ſame line, only with the letters of their Octaves prefix'd at firſt
ſight

fight palpaby, difcovering what they ftand·for.

How to alter the Octave in a Song or Lefson.

This of excellent ufe in Dialogues.

By which means the Octave only, not the Cliff is altered, neither is there the left fhadow. of the old confufion; for the *G*, which I inftanced in, or any other Note in this cafe, will ftand in every part in the fame place.   And certainly, one that has but very indifferent skill in Singing, can rife or fall an Octave, when the prefixed letter fhall give him timely warning of it.

2. If the Notes afcend, or defcend by degrees, and you have occafion to go far into another Octave, when you come to an higher *G*, alter the Signal Letter, and it falls upon the lowermoft·line; the like difcretion alfo muft be ufed in defcending: by which means, and good·fore-caft, no Song can be fo fpiteful and unlucky, but may be evidently, and conveniently

D 4   written

written in the compafs of four lines,
which is the ftatute of our Hypothefis, the lowermoft beginning with *G*,
the uppermoft ending with *F* ; and the
higher and lower Notes than thefe,
by the change of the Signal Letter,
ought to be lodged in their own
Octaves, to which they do belong.

But becaufe many Inftruments con-
tain thick and complex ftrokes, and
it would be too much to alter the
Octave upon the account of any fingle Note. It is left to the pleafure
and contrivance of the Mufick-Mafter, to ufe either four, five, or fix
lines, as his Inftrument requires;
where the afcititious lines alfo will
enjoy the benefit of our conftant
Univerfality; for the uppermoft line of
five will be always, and upon all Inftruments *A*, the uppermoft of fix *C*,
and by how many the more the lines
are, the more neceffity there is, that
they fhould be conftantly, and uni-
verfally the fame.

Now the reafon why I would advife to four lines, rather then more,
is, not only becaufe our Effay of an
Octave is compleated therein, but
that the leffer variety there is, the
more

more perspicuous they are to the eye;
which has need of all advantages we
can contrive for its help, especially in
the full speed of a quick division : But
for the lessons which are compounded
with three or four Consonant Notes
in one stroke, 'tis most convenient to
use five or six lines, and according
to the generally received custom, we
have formed all our examples in five
lines; because we desire not to contend, unless absolute necessity requires, or else there be very good
advantages to be gained thereby.

CHAP.

CHAP. V.

*The Defign applyed to Inftrumental Mu-
fick, and firft to the Violin.*

THIS way of Writing may not
feem fo very neceffary for the
Violin, as the Voice, becaufe moft
Leffons crowd themfelves into one
(*G fol re ut*) Cliff, as it is already
placed ; whereas the various parts of
the Voice did indifpenfably require
many.

But let a Mufician confider, whilft
he ftrives by that means to hook in
both the higher and lower Notes, he
gains neither conveniently ; and by
playing in his old prefcribed Compafs,
condemns this moft fpritely Mufick
to a drowfie Melancholy. Upon
which account, the *French* Muficians
already place *G* in the lower line,
(though without any thoughts or refpect to our Hypothefis) as we pro-
pofe.

All this, methinks, fhould perfwade
a man to remove his Notes one line
lower, and fpend a week or two in
practifing the fame pofition of two
different

different Octaves, whereby his leſſons
will always fall more conveniently in
the Syſteme of lines, and himſelf be
admitted into the priviledge of this
Univerſal Character ; but ſee the
Gamut both ways.

The Old.

The New.

Any Violin Leſſon of the French pricking
will serve for an example.

But when I conſider the Viol, it
more abſolutely preſſeth for relief, and
deſires it may no longer ſuffer its preſent diſtractions ; for it was never
able to ſhrink it ſelf into one Cliff, or
be

be a recreation to the Player, till he had, with more then double pains merited his pleasure.

Wherefore, since 'tis so important to be an easie delight, and 'tis the Masters interest to make it so; I would have him, after he hath asked his Scholar, whether he would learn by Notes or Letters? Ask him in the second place, whether he desires to learn his Notes in one month or two? if in two months or more, let him learn his two Cliffs with all their variations, if in one (as who desires to be kept longer in the slavish principles of a Science than he must needs) instruct him in this plain and united method : For why should you bring him unnecessarily into those perplexities, which less than the constant practice of a year can never perfect?

I have already shew'd the trouble of different Cliffs, and the clear order which arises from their union, which I omit to apply here, left I should be tedious, when my Reader's apprehensions can't but be fully satiated. Only, let me observe, how rightfully the Notes succeed one another in this alteration by Octaves; how much justice

ftice there is that *c ſol fa ut,* ſhould
come into the place of *c fa ut,* and *c
ſol fa* into his ; by which they do, as
it were, poſſeſs the very inheritance
of their Fathers: Whilſt before reaſon had no foundation to argue the
place of any Note, but by an unjuſt
uſe we were to know *b fa b mi,* in
the middle Cliff, where *c fa ut* ſtood
in the Baſe ; where alſo *Ala mi re*
was wont to juſtle it ſelf in upon the
Treble.

An

An example of a Viol Leffon, moving up and down the lower and middle Octaves.

It was altogether needlefs to infert this example, but that I would avoid the leaft fufpition; that this Effay is obfcure or unpracticable; for this is all that is to be obferved in the Writing any Viol Leffon (as might have been collected out of what I faid before, *viz.*) *The Bafe part remains here and every where elfe, the fame it was; and the Notes of the middle part are only removed from the lines, into the fpaces underneath them;* that is, the Notes ftand in the fame places as they do in the Bafe, and the Signal *M,* gives notice to play them an Octave higher. You need never alter the *B* flat, which remains ever conftant to the fame place.

And methinks, Violifts fhould become Patrons of this Propofal, not only from the allurements of conveniency, but from a grave and noble pride, that all other Mufick conforms it felf to the writing of the Bafe, which the Viol is moft concern'd in, and that part being

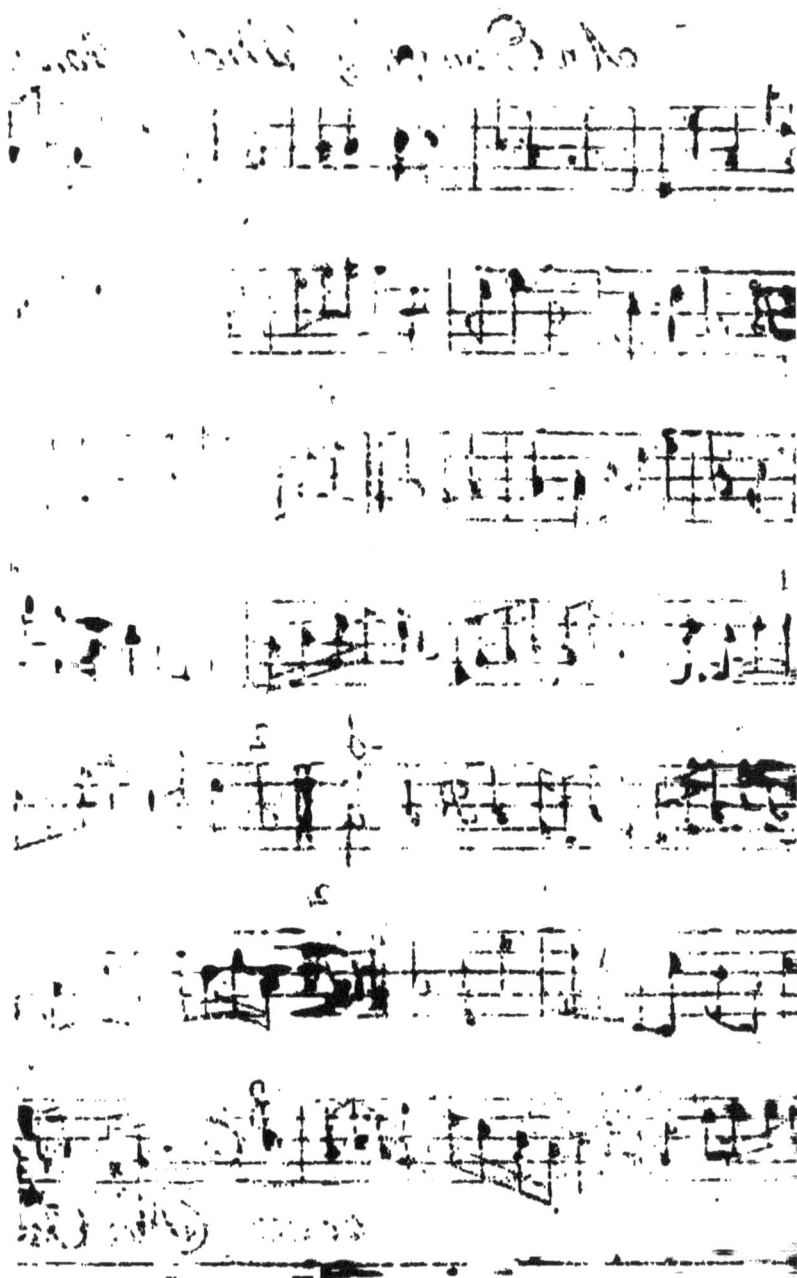

being truly the foundation to the reſt of the Muſick; it was moſt neceſſary to conform to that, in the contrivance of all our Superſtructures.

You have already ſeen the conveniency, and becauſe I would rather be troubleſom than obſcure, give me leave a little further to argue, what, and how ſmall the alteration is. For *F fa ut*, or the Baſe Cliff is the ſame it was before; and they who underſtand it, have not only advantage to be perfect in this, but alſo to play by the pricking of all other Muſick, which is to be conformable to this it's ſteady foundation. So that all the conditions we treat for, in this uniting of Muſick are, that *in the middle part the Notes ſhould be removed from the lines into the places underneath them; and in the Treble, from one line to the next immediately under; the ſpaces proportionably after the ſame manner.*

Certainly, the change is ſo inconſiderable, that I ſhould think this unworthy my pains, unleſs the difficulty was ſo great, which demands redreſs, and neceſſity required me to anſwer the perverſe obſtinacy of ſome, who would oppoſe even the juſteſt alterations;

tions; as *Quintilian* obferv'd in his days, *Vitio malignitatis humanæ, vetera femper in laude, præfentia in faftigio effe.*

But if any fhall contemn this as a fmall petite invention, becaufe it is fo ealie and natural, let them remember what a grave company of fuch contemners were baffled in fetting an egg upright upon the table, before they were fhew'd how. And I can't think that any Ingenious perfon, can impute the facility of this Propofal to its difgrace, fince I have taken care by fumming up its advantages to make it appear *as profitable as eafie.*

I have one more Effay (though independent upon the former Propofal) to make, before I difmifs the Viol, which upon many accounts hath been efteemed by many impartial and underftanding perfons. And that which gave the firft occafion of this furmife, was the odd inconvenient fituation of the Notes upon the old Viol Tuning, which with their Concords lye fo crofsly, that in all Confort we are forced to play the fingle Notes only, or elfe undergo very difficult ftops.

I

I would therefore play by Notes upon fome pleafant *Lyra* Tuning, that the moft frequent Notes be always ftruck open, that their Concords may be their neareft neighbours, and at laft the whole Viol, with an unftop'd freedom, may eccho forth a full Confort-ftroke, ufually the key of the Leffon.

And what fhould hinder, but this might be done? for all the Notes which are upon the Viol *De-Gambo*, are alfo upon the Lyra Viol, though in other places; but that thofe other places on the Lyra Tuning, are moft convenient, is proved by Mufick-Mafters themfelves, who generally fet their fweeteft Airs, and pleafanteft Suits of Leffons that way.

Whereas we are now forc'd to learn both by Notes and Letters, which are anfwered with two different Tunings, and a trouble into the bargain of the ftrings going continually out of tune; we might do (according to this Propofal) all under one.

But that which is here moft really worth our confideration, is; that if we play the moft noble and fociable.

way by Notes, the Viol is not able to exprefs its felf in its fulleft Harmony, when otherwife it might be a little Confort, within a Confort, (like the moft worthily admired, but too foft and filent Lute) it is now forc'd to grumble a difmal Bafe, which fhews neither excellency in the Player, nor any fweetnefs in the inftrument, without the treble of fome other Mufick, which is to give it life and perfection.

I make choice of this following Tuning; whofe two loweft ftrings are the fame notes they were before, the two next their Name-fakes; where the Octave Notes lye upon the fame frets, and each other ftring open, only the fecond ftring is *B*, fharp or flat as the leffon requires, and the treble *D*, as was the Fourth and Sixth ftrings.

And

The Consort Lyra tuning by Notes.

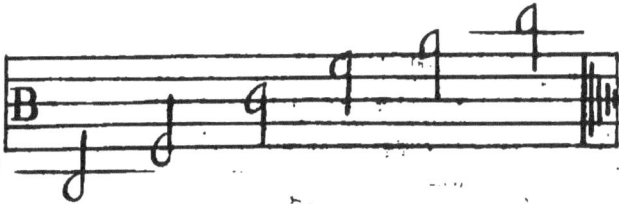

By Letters.

And fo foon as thefe are known to
be the places of the Notes upon the
Viol, you may play any ground or
divifion by fight upon this, though it
were compofed for the other tuning;
not only, becaufe they chiefly confift
of fingle Notes, which are all here
with lefs trouble to be found; but the
Confort ftrokes alfo, when they oc-
cur, are fituated in a nearer, and more
friendly neighbour-hood. So that by
this advantage, we may juftly expect
in thofe Leffons, which are compofed Note-ways for the future, a more

frequent

frequent and amorous confent of double ftrings; a full Symphony continued without diftraction of the hand, heretofore diftorted by the gripes of many a malicious ftop.

Hereby alfo may thofe Lyra Leffons (which are already to be had upon this tuning) quit their *a*, *b*, *c*, rudiments of Letters, and be underftood and honoured in the character of Notes; from whence will arife fuch an entire agreement in the practice of the Viol, as will bring the Learner to a much more early perfection.

And indeed, here lies the happinefs of this Propofal, *That you may at once have the melody of the Lyra, and yet the intelligence of Notes*; which are both equally capable of having the Graces adjoyn'd, and may be indifferently ufed upon this prefent tuning.

Though if at any time the Scholar be idle, or elfe there be fome extraordinary Leffons, confifting of many thick and full ftrokes, troublefom with the frequent occurrence of flats or fharps; you may prick them by letters, as fome Mufick-mafters already do (upon this account) their
hardeft

hardeft leffons upon the old Viol tuning.

It may be enquired, perhaps, whether or no I allow but one tuning upon an inftrument?

Yes; once at a Wedding, and upon fome unufual occafions; but then, that prefent variety, which is many times fo cauflefsly affected, I cannot but dif-allow. That Scholars, after every fuite of leffons, fhould travel into an unknown Region, to fee fafhions in another tuning (when their leffons might have been as well fet upon their old; neither do they become any wifer than before) doth not proceed either from *an Englifh conftancy or wifdom*; and is ufually defired by thofe that are fickle and unskilful, who are well recompenc'd with the trouble of tuning, which I don't grudge them. I know compofers may poffiebly contrive their leffons upon fuch keys, and beginning upon an unlucky note, may carry the air fuch a compafs up or down that it will not go with a pleafant convenience upon the common tuning; but I fpeak not of their powerful abilities and phanfies, which I would ftill have them by all means practife and pleafe themfelves in.   E 3   I

I fay therefore, for the common ufe of Mufick, efpecially among Practitioners, and in all Confort (as is already generally obferved) 'tis impertinency and wantonnefs to affect various Tunings; fince alfo thofe of the Lute and Viol here propofed, fet the inftruments at a good correfpondent pitch to the Harpfecord, that you may tune together Notes of the fame denomination. But becaufe the bignefs of inftruments are fo various, you muft not expect any conftant unmovable law for the tuning them together; yet fetting the leffon higher or lower, will be very nigh fufficient to reconcile them to a perpetual and peaceable conformity.

I would not have a flat or fharp Tuning make any difference betwixt us; for a good natur'd man would let them both go for one, fince their alteration and trouble are fo fmall, being brought to pafs by the kind complyance of the *B* ftrings, tuned up or down, as occafion requires; which you will further fee in the tuning for the Lute.

I

The Design applyed to the Organ and Harpsechord.

I come next to the Organ, Harpsechord, and Virginals, which, besides,
the fore-mention'd Difficulties, common to all other instruments, have so
many proper to themselves, that I have
known an hundred learn, and not
three by Book; so troublesom was it
always esteemed to attain. Wherefore in *Holland* they have found out an
idle Tableture of Figures, which was
invented to relieve the memory of
their Women, who after a lying in,
or the like, were wont to forget all
their Lessons, and must begin a new;
and indeed, marriage hath been ever
thought very fatal to this without-
book Musick.

Now, that I may further satisfie and
perswade my Reader, I shall a little
explain the trouble, and shew how easily it may be remedi'd; whereas we
play upon other Instruments but by
one Cliff at a time; here the perplexity is doubled, and we always use two
different together. We should divide
our soul, and employ one part to con-

E 4   sider

fider the right hand, the other the
left; and indeed, in fuch a various and
diftracting pofition of the Notes, which
are to be at once confidered; a man
doth as neceffarily need two heads, as
two hands to play with.

And then if you talk of changing
the Clift (as many good Leffons do
frequently require) give me a man of
three or four heads; for on the left
hand, the lowermoft line, which was
G; is immediately transformed into
D; thus alfo is the right difquieted
with another different alteration; neither when you have thus far paffed the
pikes, will you find any reft or fettle-
ment, but all the lines and fpaces will
become any thing, by the arbitrary
and tyrannical power of *C fol fa ut*;
which, if you confider, is required to
be done at a fudden upon fix lines; I
believe it is fufficient to appale the
warmeft confidence; and could a Mafter but rightly inftruct his Scholar to
apprehend fo terrible an intricacy,
without doubt, it were enough to cure
an Ague, and which is all (as I know)
it would be good for.

Now in the way here propofed, he
hath the fame univerfal law for both
                                    hands,

hands, *G* is always the lower line, and fo forward the fame for ever in the Bafe and Treble: And if at any time the right hath occafion to defcend, or the left to move upwards, it is but altering the fignal Letter of the O-ctave, and without any trouble, you may play in what place, and with what hand you pleafe; becaufe every particular Octave hath fuch a different profpect, and fyfteme within it felf. That you will find but very little inconveniency, when you fhift your writing by eight Notes, which lie round about, and come over again fo much the fame, that I take the keys of an Harpfechord to be an exact emblem of our Hypothefis, as we before explained it; and confequently they be moft fuitable to that method they fo much refemble.

The Plate for an example of the Harpfecord.

And here I expect to fall into the unmerciful hands of an Objecter, who would undo me all at once, becaufe I alter my Octaves, as often as he do's his Cliffs.

But

But to satisfie him, and save my self, I suppose, it will be sufficient, if I prove, that every thing remains the same, and so our alteration be as good as none at all.

1. In our movement by Octaves, all the lines and spaces do ever remain possessed of the same Notes. *Archimedes's* Engine, with which he thought himself able to move the world, had he but footing out of it; is much too weak to stir *G* from the lowest line, or disorder any of the rest from their fixed settlement.

2. The Keys signifyed by those Notes, are specifically and in kind, though not individually the same, which is so very equivalent, both in shew and reality, that I dare trust my cause to any ones serious observations; but to help his thoughts, let him consider how the jacks of an Harpsecord are ready cut out into Octaves, and have the very face and eyes of our proposal. As for example, betwixt every eight Keys, there are placed three sharps, and two sharps, which the sight apprehends together, as the entire Systeme of an Octave; when therefore you see a Note placed

upon

upon the middle line of five, it fignifies the key betwixt the two fharps, and if *Tr* is placed before the Note, then the key betwixt the two upper fharps is intended ; if *M*, the key betwixt the two middle fharps, if *B*, that between the two lower, and fo of the reft, which is the only alteration I require. And who can here find in their hearts to be quarrelfom and unkind, when I fave them fo much, and put them to fo little trouble? As that *Almain* I have inftanced in, cannot be pricked in the way now ufed under eight lines, mine requires but five.

And for the fatisfaction of any, how much the feveral Octaves both appear, and are the fame, let them but begin their leffons eight keys inclufively, higher or lower then they learn'd them, and they fhall find themfelves able to play them, as far as the compafs of the inftrument will permit; but if any fhou'd be put out by their fancy, let them fet their hands right, and fhut their eyes, and I'le warrant them they do it.

It muft not be expected that this will fall out fo very pat on other Inftruments, except in the Tuning of the

Viol

Viol laſt propoſed; neither is it my fault, for I have not undertaken to alter the ſituation of the Notes upon the Inſtruments, but in the Book; that the Reader muſt all along remember that this propoſal is only concerning the Orthography of Muſick, it's performance and harmony remaining untouch'd.

The Lute hath always had an undeniable ſoveraignty over other inſtrumental Muſick, ſince that it ſelf is a compleat Conſort, ſounding with ſuch a ſoft, but powerful ſweetneſs, as if it were well acquainted with all the intrigues of the mind; ſometimes diſarming anger, and with its gentle breath, cooling a revengeful rage; ſometimes, by a contrary power it kindles a delightful flame, and raiſes a kinder, but no leſs fiery paſſion; as it is obſerved, that Muſick doth always promote that humour, which a man is moſt inclined to; though there are alſo ſeveral leſſons, which in their own nature have a greater tincture of mirth or melancholy.

But upon what account ſoever it is, you may obſerve the Lute to be in ſo

great

great efteem among all Romancers, that they never make mention of any other Mufick, than this with the Voice; for if they can but get a moments leifure to place their Heroes in an arbour, amidft the green Ornaments of the Spring; they prefent them with a Lute to Court thofe Miftreffes, all the world knows they have deferved, but are at laft forced to ufe this overcomnig Mufick, as being of proportionate power to charm, with that of their prodigious fwords to conquer.

And even the grave Philofophers themfelves have fo great a reverence for it, that their Mufical experiments are always quoted in the name of a Lute-ftring.

But the Lute is fo generally acknowledged fupream, that it is as needlefs for me to prove it, as it is impertinent to my purpofe; wherefore, we will now only enquire, what concerns it has in our prefent propofal; though, indeed, the Tableture, by which we play upon the Lute, is fo convenient, that except a Scholar knows the Notes already by underftanding other Mufick, or elfe hath fome further defign of Compofing, he may poffibly
content

content himself with that practical writing.

Yet since the building is so high and noble, who would not take a little more pains to lay a better foundation ? we must spend some years in attaining it, and many more in the enjoyment; and shall we never come to so much perfection, as to understand what this Musick is that pleases us so well ?

And if we consider it, the difficulty will not be found sufficient to countermand such great conveniencies, as will flow from hence; for if one can but tell how the *Gamut* is situated (as the next cut explains it) he may write out any treble upon the Lute ; and a little more knowledge will contrive a Base. Now if a Scholar should make no further progress than this, yet it would be a pritty accomplishment to be able to set a Tune.

And for one that is well versed in Notes, it is much better to play his Lessons writ in this kind, for he doth not only get a particular light into the composition of his Lessons, but continually perfects that way, which is common to all his Musick.

I

I confess, when it was necessary to manage the Lute in two or three different Cliffs (like the old way for the Harpsechord) it was too troublesom to undertake, and too private a design to be concern'd in ; but since the Lute is reconciled to it self and all other Instruments, that by an united acquaintance, and happy league, they assist to one another's attainment; it is a most general interest to practise it by Notes.

Because few or none at present, write their Lute lessons by Notes, I have taken liberty to propose such a Scheme, as I could possibly contrive with the most convenience and perspicuity.

It must be considered, that the Lute (being it self a Consort) is of very great compass, and contains two Octaves, besides the Base ; so that there must be a Mean and Treble, which may be successively placed upon a Systeme of four or five lines, by the alteration of the signal letters, and that without any great trouble, either to write or understand ; because the change is by Octave Notes, which once known upon the Lute, will be

eafily

eafily found upon the book, where the name-fake Notes have all the fame pofition.

There muft be a time, before you can tell the ftrings open, by the names of Treble, Second, Third, &c. and the Alphabet of ftopped frets; now a little more time would perfect the *Gamut,* and I am confident 'tis altogether as eafie a way, when one is firft of all to begin.

Now for the Bafe, becaufe the time of it is known by the Note, under which it ftands, and will do well enough, if fo be we ftrike it with the ftring appointed, which is all the direction we have, now-adays, given us. As alfo, that 'tis not fo frequently ftrucken, as to deferve a Syfteme of lines to it felf. I have refolved the Notes of the Bafe, into their own fignificative letters, which are much more plain to be underftood, then if they lodged up and down the lines and fpaces.

And in this I am fure, the now Tableture hath not the better of me; for why fhould not *E e* (that is double *E la mi*) fignifie the twelfth, which Note it is, as well as a figure of five, 5 ?

or *G* the tenth, as well as an *A* with three heavy ſtrokes upon his back.

Surely that is moſt natural and eaſie; but why a figure of five ſhould ſtand for the Twelfth, and a figure of four for the Eleventh, I could not a long time underſtand the Etymology, till at laſt I remembred there was ſix lines for the ſix firſt ſtrings, under which the poor Seventh ſtandeth without ever a ſtroke; but how unjuſtly, let them anſwer, that originally robbed him of it; though, for my part, I believe, it was done with a good intent for ſaving a ſtroke: well then, do but ſuppoſe the *A* that is abſent, and five ſtrokes to be added to the Seventh, and there's a lawful Twelfth ſterling; which is a conceit, I confeſs, that though a man had thought on it before he went to bed, yet he might poſſibly have never dream'd on it all night; neither, indeed, is it to be remembred by a young beginner at once telling.

Wherefore all the odds, I know, betwixt the letters I have propoſed, and thoſe old figured Baſes, are, that

F   any

any Mufician may underftand what my written Bafe means; but the other is fome private conjuring of a Lutinift.

When the Notes of the middle part are to be ftruck with the thumb, I have noted them with the fmaller letters of the Alphabet; as you have an example in *Arrons Jig*, which are there affociated to the Treble, to make a convenient fatisfaction for the abfence of the farther diftant Bafe.

Here infert the Plate for the Gamut *upon the Lute, and* Arrons Jig.

I have chofe this tuning, not only as 'tis that which the moft excellent Lutinift, Mr. *John Rogers* ordinarily teaches in *London* to his Scholars; but alfo, becaufe the Notes lye here in their moft natural pofition, as you may find by computing their diftances one from another; to which the Tuning of the ftrings does exactly agree. Only obferving that, *F fa ut*, is ufually fharp in this, as in many other keys, where *Mi* is not difplaced by a *b* flat.

r

I know many make the eighth ſtring *Gamut*, and the fourth, *G ſol re ut*, but a little conſideration will ſatisfie them, it cannot be ſo here; for when we alter the Lute to a flat Tuning, we let down the fourth and the eighth; now the firſt *b* flat doth not uſe to ſtand upon *G*, but *B*; whereas, therefore, they make the fourth ſtring *G*, and the tuning ſhews *Mi* to be placed there, it muſt needs be falſe; and the fourth, by right, be aſſigned to *B*, which is the very country where *Mi* was bred and born.

This is alſo proved by the tuning of the Baſes; for it is but half a Note from the eighth to the ſeventh, which by their account will happen betwixt *G* and *A*, but by ours, betwixt *B* and *C*, according to their juſt diſtance in a ſharp tuning.

One thing may ſeem to thwart our deſign of playing on the Lute by Notes, which is, that ſeveral ſuits of leſſons require different tunings, and will thence breed a confuſion, becauſe the ſame ſtring will not always be the ſame Note.

F 2 And

And indeed, this argument may as well be urged againſt playing by Notes upon any Inſtrument that hath divers tunings; wherefore this one propoſed, is to ſerve for Conſort, and all ordinary occaſions; and this I ſay, from a deſire not to contend, for I know there is ſufficient variety upon this one tuning, and as good ſuits of leſſons as ever were play'd upon any.

But you muſt remember that under this one tuning, I comprehend both ſharp and flat, which gain ſuch advantage by altering the tuning of ſome ſtrings, that you can't but be pleaſed with the conſideration.

For, firſt, in the alteration of Baſes, we do not change them from one whole Note to another; but ſometimes the flat Notes are made ſharp, and ſometimes the ſharp are turned into flat.

Now, whereas otherwiſe we have a ſharp or flat prefixed at the beginning of a line or ſpace, and are forced all along to remember, that whenſoever a Note occurs thereon, it muſt be
ſtopped

ftopped according to its prefixt quali-
fication; here we need only ftrike the
Note, and by the tuning, 'tis provided
to be true.

Thus, inftead of a continual *B* flat,
we tune down the eighth, the fourth,
and the Treble, which will require
you to obferve; that as when a *B* flat
was placed upon a line, all the Notes
upon that line were ftopped a fret
lower; fo here the ftring being tuned
half a Note lower, all the Notes upon that ftring will fall a fret higher.

Hence *K* fret, which is hardly ever
ufed upon the fharp tuning, is upon the
treble in the flat tuning, *G fol re ut*
it felf; but this trouble is only upon
that one ftring, and that one ftop of
C fol fa ut upon the Fourth.

And now we may difmifs the Lute,
having in our Scheme affigned places
to all its Notes, whofe compafs it cannot exceed; for though the Viol
would oftentimes fally forth to the
utmoft inch of finger-board, yet this
never condefcends to move below the
frets, and therefore will be obedient to
the lines and fpaces allotted.

F 3 Having

Having thus explain'd my Hypothefis, fhew'd its conveniency, and applyed it in particular to the moft con-
fiderable Mufick ; I come now to an-
fwer thofe Objections, which may feem
to contradict it.

CHAP.

CHAP. VI.

The Objections Answered.

Obj. I. I Firſt of all meet with ſome peeviſh piece of Antiquity, that commends only the Golden days of his youth, and is now weary of the world, and the world of him ; but if there be any good in it, 'tis that which he received from his fore-fathers, and not what this degenerating age hath corrupted.

He therefore defies our *preſent innovation*, and abhors ſuch a *confuſion*, as would bring the Notes of *C ſol fa ut cliff*, from the ſpaces wherein they were placed, and ſet them upon the lines underneath, which was never yet known.

Anſw. I. *Innovation is either of that which is bad, or that which is good* ; if then this be bad or inconvenient, rejeƈt it upon its own account ; if good, what hinders but it ſhould be embraced ? and prythee tell me, if a Scholar ſhall learn in half the time others have done, will he much care f they call him Innovatour ? why ſhould

not

not we accept an *Univerfal Character*
in Mufick, as Arithmaticians have
done that noble way of accompting
by *Decimal Fractions*, where all things
are brought to one Catholick nume-
ration?

Anf. II. Confufion is when things
are different and perplex'd ; method,
when they all agree and are united.
Now I leave it to an impartial Reader,
which upon this account ought to be
cenfured *this way or that.*

Object. II. The Cliffs always ftand
in a line, for they are five Notes afunder, if therefore in the Bafe you fet
F fa ut upon the line, and in the
middle part *C fol fa ut* in the fpace,
you make them but four Notes diftant, which is falfe Mufick ; and be-
fides, that very Numerical, *G fol re
ut,* which ftood in the uppermoft
fpace of one five lines; in the next
five lines, will be in the loweft line.

Anfw. I can hardly think any one
will be fo dull, to read thus far, and
then make this Objection; but left
any one fhould ftill run droaning in
his

his own way, I shall mind him of
ours, and tell him again, we do not
reckon upwards, as if the lines were
continued together; neither make we
any Cliffs five Notes afunder, but
we compleat an Octave in the Syfteme of four lines, which reaches to
F fa ut, and then begin the Syfteme
of the next four lines, in the middle
part, with *G* again; as after Saturday
night comes Sunday morning.

But then, if for conveniency of
pricking we allow the Syfteme to be
of five or fix lines, why muft he fall
to his old continuation? for herein
the Notes of any higher Octave are
Exoticks, taken in only ftranger-
wife for their trade and commerce;
and therefore muft not be looked
upon as at home; neither is it neceffary they fhould, for he that plays,
minds only the part before him, not
what the Bafe was, or the Treble
might be, but what his prefent task
is; and fhould he look after more,
he will find a dearer fympathy of the
agreeing parts in this, than in any o-
ther way of writing.

Object.

Object. III. Are we not already provided with a way that will do ? and are not Muficians verfed therein ? would you have them forego their former pains, and take as much more only to the fame purpofe ?

Anfw. For thofe who have attain'd that laborious, but unneceffary excellency, let them, if they pleafe, enjoy it. But if there be a nearer and eafier way, why fhould not thofe Guides be fo honeft to lead us in it ? Muft every poor School-boy run the rifquo of his Mafter's antiquated ftudies? And truly, if Mufick-mafters will continue obftinate, to maintain fuch needlefs difficulties, they may, like fome (Muficians heretofore) be left to play by themfelves in *Fidlers Ifland.*

We have the experience of the former age, and our own too; that ftanding upon the fhoulders of our Anceftors, we may furely fee further than they, and difcover what they never faw; if then there be a fhorter cut, why muft we go about ?

Suppofe

Suppose the old project was brought to pass, that the nook of Land, which joins *Africa* to the continent of *Asia*, was divided, and so a passage out of the *Mediterranean*, opened into the Red Sea; would the Apprentices of all former Merchants be ever obliged, when they took a Voyage to the *East-Indies*, to measure the same wide circuit their Masters did; to double the cape of good Hope, twice cross the scorching line, and suffer even the Southern cold, when they might return in less than half the time by the Streights of *Gibralter*? And with no less folly, must Musicians be still condemned to steer their wandring course through many Cliffs, because their Predecessors went that way before them.

Object. IV. But certainly, the design must be very forc'd and unnatural, which shall oblige all Instruments of such different shapes and compass, and way of utterance, to the same manner of writing, and that too clouded in the darkest obscurity, by the abrogation of Cliffs, which are the only directions to inform us where any Note stands. *Answ.*

Anf. Though Inftruments are various, yet allMufick is fundamentallythe fame; there is the fame beloved interval betwixt all confonant ftrokes, the fame perpetual Oeconomy of an Octave wherefoever it dwells, that all our feveral Mufick is but the fame kind of harmonious foul embodied in different fhapes; for if it were otherwife, the fame leffon could not be play'd upon feveral Inftruments. Wherefore, though their ftops and ftrikings be various, but the thing the fame which is to be ftopped or ftruck upon them; 'tis evident that one way of writing may be fufficient.

As if there was a common Character for a horfe; from thence a *Frenchman* would call it *Cheval,* a *Dutchman, Pfert, &c.* For the thing being once known which is reprefented to them, they would from the fame character exprefs it according to the different dialect of their Nations.

And thus the tune of all Mufick confifting in the fame Notes, and the fame

fame method of Notes; why may they not have the fame fituation, and be reduced to one univerfal chara-&er ? which allowing the latitude of four Octaves, is fpatious enough for the widelt compafs of any Inftrument; and more might be granted if occafion does require.

And then for abolifhing Cliffs, it is very reafonable, that their perplexity and variety being taken away, they themfelves fhould alfo perifh; which is fo far from caufing obfcurity, that 'tis the very thing which makes it clear and eafie : For is it not much better to have *G* always the lowelt line, than to have an informing Cliff to tell you, it is fometimes *G*, fome-times *F*, fometimes *E*, and fo to di-ftinguifh what it is upon every parti-cular occafion where it varies.

If then an univerfal and conftant order be not moft plain and intelligi-ble! if this be a wonder! I'le give any man leave to cry out——— *Help me, Ralpho, with thy Prophetick Spirit; Deliver me Bacchus from thy dozy fumes:*

fumes: Pity me ye confounded Sons of Nimrod, *that I muſt ſtill ſuffer the curſe of my old confuſed diſorders.*

Object. V. But will not Muſick hereby become common and contemptible, proſtituted--- - *to the weak and rabble?* and be no longer the delight of Princes, but the mean paſtime of the vulgar.

Anſw. Which if this Eſſay be guilty of, 'tis a contradiction to cry out of it's obſcurity ; but I anſwer.

Since that Muſick is no jugling, cheat, or empty toy, but an innocent and ſubſtantial pleaſure, a natural branch of one of the moſt noble Sciences ; it fears not to diſcover it ſelf to any, and being of the liberal Arts, humbly admits acceſs to the meaneſt admirer. For they the more generally known they are, the more excellent they appear; and upon this account, the moſt Ingenious and Learned Men I meet with, are always moſt liberal and communicative of their knowledge: And this they do without

out any prejudice, nay, with the greateſt advantage to themſelves; for there
is ſo great a depth in all Learning,
that they do thereby only diſpoſe
people better to underſtand and ad-
mire their excellencies.

And particularly in Muſick, there
are ſuch various, ſuch large accompliſhments, that will ſuit every ones
quality and capacity. A brisk and
lively Air will penetrate the thickeſt
skull, and actuate the dulleſt ruſtick
with joy and dancing : But then there
are Quires of Conſort for nobler entertainments, above both the skill and
charges of the common people.

And were Muſick in more frequent
uſe, we ſhould not ſee it more deſpiſed,
but more generally eſteemed; *'Tis cu-*
ſtom makes it underſtood, and brings it
into reputation. Thus when every
Swain had his rural ditty, and the
Shepherds ſate Singing their Eclogs
on the Plains of *Peleponneſus*, than did
the *Athenian Princes* love and honour
theſe Muſical delights : And *Epami-*
nondas himſelf, that renowned Cap-
tain

tain of *Thebes*, learned both to play
and sing of his Master *Denny* ; (as *Cornelius Nepos* thought it worthy to report among the great actions of his
life.)

Was ever Mathematicks contemned, because a Carpenter understood
his Rule ? or fair Writing under-valued, because many ordinary persons
more excel in it, than Noblemen and
great Scholars? neither will Musick
be cast away, because performed by
the hands of the vulgar.

I should not have been so long in
confuting an Objection, which is so
plain a mistake, but that upon this account some have so stomached this
Essay : And since they do so urge me,
I don't care, if I do fall under the dint
of their Argument, *viz. That Musick
is hereby exposed to the world habitable————that it may possibly be more
generally practised, and a perfection
sooner attained by the learner.*

Object. VI. But what shall become
of the lessons already written ? or
when we come amongst them of the
old

old way, how shall we Confort with them?

Anf. Many Scholars would be glad to arrive at this objection; if they could play all that was fet them, they would think themfelves well enough. But this is not all, for they may be able to play any Bafe by fight, which is the fame it was before; and for other quicker leffons, (which are feldom performed without practice) any fervant may tranfcribe them, who though he cannot practice for his Mafter, and transfer his skill, he can his writing.

And though this fhould be a trouble for the prefent, yet time will quickly abolifh it; the daily compofing and learning new leffons, wipe away the old ones; fo that fuch alterations in Mufick as this, already have, and may as well now find this inconveniency infenfible.

And for tranfcribing leffons out of the old, into this new method, there remains no difficulty, 'tis but (as I faid

G before)

before) removing the Notes of the middle part out of the spaces, into the lines underneath them, and in the treble to set *G* in the lowest line. But Scholars need not trouble them-selves for this, no Master will be so dif-ingenious, but upon their entrea-ties, to direct them this way. And I have heard the most eminent, Master *Theodorus Stefkins*, and Mr. *Matthew Lock*, (whose excellent compolitions I can't but tell the world, how I ad-mire) affirm, we might use this way if we pleafed; the former of which, once tranfcribed for me the Song, which I have given you for an exam-ple, according to this prefent propo-fal.

I have now paffed the Objections, and made a shift to efcape alive; but becaufe I have been fo long engaged in them, I am willing to give the Reader fome account thereof.

It muft be expected when any thing is propofed entirely new (as this is the firft attempt was ever made of this kind in Mufick) it fhould appear a little ftrange and furprifing; and therefore our

our former and more acquainted notions of things, which have already poſſeſſion of our minds, ſuggeſt all manner of Objections to keep out any new intruding propoſal: And I have upon this account been frequent in diſcourſe with perſons converſant in Muſick, that underſtanding their ſuggeſtions, I might in ſome ſort allay the heats of their ſurprizal. Neither do I think this argumentative method is more litigious than profitable ; for I have always found my ſelf better able to underſtand any *Phænomenon* by reading ſuch Authors that contraverted it, rather than thoſe that only laid down the direct definition.

I would not therefore have my Reader terrified at theſe objected difficulties, not for their number, becauſe they are for the moſt part but ſome ſhie ſurmiſes, which better acquaintance, and more familiarity, will eaſily wear away ; nor for their largeneſs, which I purpoſely deſigned, that by the more exact ſearch and enquiry therein, every particular might be more throughly apprehended.

G 2 So

So that this design being acquitted of its late impeachments, comes more boldly with its two old arguments to claim acceptance, *viz.*

1. *By assuring its favourers a remission of more than half their task in the tedious principles.*

2. *And an universal knowledge and practice, from the common pricking of all sorts of Musick.*

So that I have nothing more, but to sum up my accounts, and conclude with a compendious narration of the whole.

nol

The Conclusion.

I Come now to review a Learners proceedings, which as they lye in the dark, are thought difficult and tirefome; whereas, if he had a fhort Landskip of his pleafant journey, and always in his eye a profpect of his defired end, the way it felf would be fatisfaction, and his practice only a continued pleafure.

His firft bufinefs is a perfect knowledge of the feven Letters, and I think none undertake Mufick, but are thus far skill'd in their Alphabet.

Then he muft know the feven particular places, to which thefe Letters do belong, as G for the loweft line, A for the firft fpace, B for the next line, and fo forwards; whofe refpective feats upon the Inftrument being known and applyed to the book, render him capable to exprefs the *Tune* of any leffon; and for the *Time*, after you have underftood the comprehenfive value of each Note; 'tis but a knack to ftamp

at

at every Emphatical Note, and (as a jefting obferver of the motion of the foot told me) a man will be thorowpac'd in the Mufical amble.

And this is all that is requifite to play in Confort, which without doubt may be brought to pafs in a little time, by frequent practice, and the conduct of a *skilful Mafter.*

To whofe judgment I readily fubmit any thing this Effay hath propofed, not only, becaufe a ftander by may perceive more, than he who manages the Game ; but alfo one whofe employment it is, may be better able to emprove it, than one who takes it up only for a diverfion.

Wherefore if a Lute-mafter fhall think it more convenient to ufe two Syftemes of lines, inftead of thofe Letters for the Bafe Octave ; or any Mufician (for the reafons alledged) conceive it more diftinct to ufe but four lines in a Syfteme, or the like ; I fhall moft readily comply with any thing their judgment and experience fhall find beft.   Let

Let them, to whom it belongs, have
the honour of it's perfection; it fuffi-
ceth me to be inftrumental to its advancement; which cannot but be pro-
moted, *by abrogating the perplexed va-*
riety of Cliffs, and eftablifhing all Mu-
fick in one conftant and univerfal order,
by the foundation law of Octaves.

As I think it of abfolute neceffity
for a beginner to have one to inftruct
him, fo in my judgment, it will be
certainly moft advantageous for him
to make choice of fuch an one, as be-
gins at the bottom, and leads him the
moft underftanding way; to inftruct
him (for inftance) that an Octave is a
compleat Cycle of Mufick, that all the
intermediate Notes, in their natural
pofition, are two half Notes diftant,
except *C* and *F*, which when he knew
where, he would alfo know why they
were fo placed; and thence underftand
the nature of Flats and Sharps; he
would apprehend the difpofition of
his Inftrument, and collect the reafon
of its tuning. He that takes fuch a
courfe as this, *viz.* to be inftructed in
the Fundamentals of Mufick, may

(per-

(perhaps) be thought to go the most difficult and furtheft way about; but they will at last find it, much the nearest way home.

But why must we now Sacrifice to *Hercules*, and hang up our imperfect Trophees upon his Pillars? we are arrived ('tis true) at the ufual boundaries of a learner's knowledge; but the glory and fatisfaction, the triumphing perfection is still behind.

'Tis an incomparable pleafure to play an Airy Tune, or well contriv'd Confort; but to be Author of it, is a kind of unknown delight. I have heard many Scholars, in vain, importune their Mafters for fome directions to this purpofe, that they would crown their pains and joys, with this last confummating kindnefs.

Whofe *Charity*, notwithftanding has been fo ftraight, or elfe their *ignorance* fo obftinate, that thofe juft entreaties were fruftrated.

I would therefore a little plead this
                                    caufe

caufe with the skilful Mufician, and fee whether it would not be a fmall trouble, yet a great advantage for him to comply: For with what eafe might he explain *Simpfon*'s Compendium, and by reducing it all along to practice, and delightful examples, drive on pleafantly through the very intricacies of compofition.

Did but a Scholar underftand the mode of leffons, the fmooth nature of a Treble, the proper movements of a leaping Bafe; how Confort is generally by Fifths, Thirds, and Eights, with fome few directions for their ufe; he needs no more but to fancy what he would write down, and write down what he fancies.

Thefe things of themfelves lye fomething deep and obfcure; but if they were undertaken by a good Mufical Ingenuity, and affifted by the directions of a learned Mafter, may be quickly brought to pafs, both with eafe and pleafure.

And I cannot think what reafon any
Inge-

Ingenuous Mufician can have to be fhie herein, for his labour would then be a continual exercife of his chiefeft excellency, and his employment only to manifeft his learning ; whereas, now he is ranck'd in the fame order with thofe Empyrical Traders, who have a parcel of Mufical Receipts, but underftand not one Note of their compofure.

The world would hereby more know and value his worth, and fo he would be feparated from the difefteemed crowd of the lower rank, and live, and be efteemed like a Mafter of an ingenious profeffion.

'Tis ftrange that fo many arguments muft be urged to perfwade men to embrace their own intereft ; but after all, methinks, a defire to fee Mufick advanced, fhould be fomething prevalent with them. For it might then come to pafs, that inftead of drinking, or fome fuch entertainments and ligaments of company, a Mufical Confort might be introduced, which would be much more happy and innocent : How would it refemble vertue and charity,

if

if the fubject of a merry meeting was *Harmony* it felf? and neighbouring Gentlemen made their mutual Treatments of that Mufick, which their own Fancies compofed, and their own hands performed? This would not impair the Mufick-mafters livelyhood, but bring him more into requeft, make his employment more conftant, and that too in the heights and excellencies of Mufick; for it can't be fuppofed, that Gentlemen fhould ever arrive fo far, without fome to inftruct them.

And thus far we may extend the bounds of Practical Mufick, which are laid upon fuch a noble foundation in the Mathematicks; that as there is fcarcely any thing there more intricate, fo there is nothing more ingenious than this.

Many an induftrious Scholar ftudies the Trigonometry of Signs and Tangents; only that he may erect a Sun-Dial, or take the right afcention of a Star, which perhaps he hath never occafion afterwards to practife; who, if Mufically inclined, may as well favour
his

his Genius therein; since the same kind
of studies might satisfie him in the Harmonical Division of an Octave, and
discover to him how the agreeing concords oblige themselves to observe
their Arithmetical laws. What prety
Philosophy there is in the vibration
of strings, and how each various stroke
is at last reconciled by an uniting coin-
cidence.

But this is so far from our Practical
Proposal, that it may suffice to have
given these hints, and so withdraw,
lest while I plead for Musick, as a noble
and lawful divertisement, it should be
found guilty of encroaching upon
those more serious studies, to which it
is to be only a recreation.

F I N I S.

ALL forts of Mufick Books and Inftruments, Lutes, Viols, Violins, Gittars, Flageolets, Caftenets, &c. with great choice of ftrings.

As alfo the beft Confort, Suits of Leffons, and the Neweft Airs ready prickt according to this Univerfal Character.

Are to be fold by John Carr, *at the* Middle-Temple-Gate.